YANKEE TAVERN

BY STEVEN DIETZ

★

★

DRAMATISTS
PLAY SERVICE
INC.

NOTE ON BILLING

The world premiere of YANKEE TAVERN was produced by
Florida Stage in Manalapan, FL, opening on May 15, 2009,
Louis Tyrrell, Producing Director; Nancy Barnett, Managing Director.

The rolling world premiere of YANKEE TAVERN was partially funded by the National New Play Network's Continued Life of New Plays Fund and was produced by Florida Stage, Curious Theatre Company (Denver) and New Jersey Repertory Company.

YANKEE TAVERN was originally commissioned by McCarter Theatre, Princeton, NJ,
Emily Mann, Artistic Director; Jeffrey Woodward, Managing Director.

SPECIAL NOTE ON SONGS/RECORDINGS

for Sarah Jane Leigh
with many years of gratitude

ACKNOWLEDGMENTS

The author wishes to acknowledge the following organizations and individuals who made additional contributions to the creation and development of YANKEE TAVERN:

McCarter Theatre Center, Princeton, NJ
Capital Hill Arts Center (CHAC), Seattle, WA
National New Play Network
John Guare
Emily Mann
Mara Isaacs
Liz Engelman
Sheila Daniels
Matthew Kwatinetz
Ed Herendeen
Joe Hanreddy
Sean Graney
Lee Sellars

AUTHOR'S NOTES

NOTE ON TEXT: The notation "overlapping" means that the speaking character continues — *without interruption* — from the end of his/her own previous speech. When *not specifically marked* in this manner, overlapping is *not* intended.

NOTE ON PACE/TONE: Though this play can be approached and rehearsed as a drama — in performance it must be played as *a thriller:* on its toes, the pace and comedy sharp, the push and consequences of the *current moment* taking precedence over the lingering losses of the past.

NOTE ON MUSIC: The premiere production of this play featured haunting and evocative musical and environmental sounds — used *sparingly and selectively* — to underscore the feel of a "thriller." No recognizable pop music should be used except for the final song from the jukebox.

YANKEE TAVERN received its world premiere at Florida Stage (Louis Tyrrell, Producing Director; Nancy Barnett, Managing Director) in Manalapan, Florida, on May 15, 2009. It was directed by Michael Bigelow Dixon. The set design was by Richard Crowell; the costume design was by Leslye Menshouse; the lighting design was by Michael Jon Burris; the sound design was by Matt Kelly; the dramaturgy was by Jonathan Wemette; and the stage manager was James Dansford. The cast was as follows:

ADAM .... Antonio Amadeo
JANET .... Kim Morgan Dean
RAY .... William McNulty
PALMER .... Mark Zeisler

This production of YANKEE TAVERN was a National New Play Network "rolling premiere," made possible by the Continued Life of New Plays Fund. The other participating theatres were Curious Theatre Company (Denver, CO), New Jersey Repertory Company (Long Branch, NJ), and Actor's Theatre of Charlotte (Charlotte, NC).

YANKEE TAVERN was subsequently produced by the Contemporary American Theatre Festival (Ed Herendeen, Producing Director; Peggy McKowen, Associate Producing Director) in Shepherdstown, West Virginia, on July 10, 2009. This production was directed by Liesl Tommy. The set design was by Robert Klingelhoefer; the costume design was by Devon Painter; the lighting design was by John Ambrosone; the sound design was by David Remedios; and the stage manager was Lori M. Doyle. The cast was as follows:

ADAM .... Eric Sheffer Stevens
JANET .... Anne Marie Nest
RAY .... Anderson Matthews
PALMER .... John Lescault

A staged reading of the play (with the title CITY OF GHOSTS) was presented as part of Florida Stage's "1st Stage" program in March 2007. It was directed by Liz Engelman.

YANKEE TAVERN (under the title CITY OF GHOSTS) was originally commissioned by the McCarter Theatre Center (Emily Mann, Artistic Director; Jeffrey Woodward, Managing Director).

CHARACTERS

ADAM — a graduate student, late twenties.

JANET — Adam's fiancée, late twenties.

RAY — a resident of the bar, sixties.

PALMER — a man, forties.

PLACE

New York City. The Yankee Tavern: an old neighborhood joint, housed on the ground floor of a decaying, abandoned, once-upon-a-time hotel. Not big. A handful of stools around the battered wooden bar. A few unremarkable tables nearby. An old vintage jukebox that no longer works. Spent neon and dusty memorabilia. This is a place that no doubt shone in the forties, but now is doling out its final shots before the crash of the wrecking ball.

TIME

2006.

Once a person was asked to step into this brutal century, anything could happen.

—John Kennedy Toole, *A Confederacy of Dunces*

YANKEE TAVERN

ACT ONE

Morning. Lights up fast.

Adam is taking chairs off the tables, stocking coolers, etc., opening up the tavern for the day, as —

Janet sits at a table, her jacket still on, staring hard at a large Starbucks coffee cup in front of her.

ADAM. *(With a grin.)* Is there something you want me to say?
JANET. See, that's it —
ADAM. It feels like there's some *one thing* you want me to say —
JANET. — That's what you do!
ADAM. — And if I can just say that to you, then everything will be *fine.* What is it, Janet? What's the thing you want me to say? *(She gives him a long look, then turns away once again.)* Things are taking shape, right? The invitations have been sent out, and the —
JANET. *(Sarcastic, not angry.)* The invitations have *not* been sent out. The save-the-date cards have gone out, but not the invitations —
ADAM. Okay, but still — we're moving forward —
JANET. — And half of yours came *back.*
ADAM. What?
JANET. The addresses you gave me — friends, family on your side — about half the save-the-date cards I sent to your list came back — *(Perhaps she removes a stack of these returned cards from her bag.)* saying, "No Such Person," "No Such Address." Why would that happen, Adam?
ADAM. I don't know — it's weird.

JANET. That's what I thought, so I called your mom — she was really glad to hear from me —
ADAM. Janet —
JANET. — Since she never hears from *you.*
ADAM. — Please leave my mother out of our marriage.
JANET. Anyway, we had a little chat and come to find out, you *made those people up.* Those cards that came back to me: made-up people!
ADAM. You love big weddings — lots of invitations, some huge production —
JANET. Adam, I never once said —
ADAM. — And so Ray and I were sitting here one morning — you know Ray, he does *way better* with the world that's *in his mind* — and so we just sort of started inventing … a few … *people. (Janet lifts one of the envelopes.)*
JANET. Robbie Marx — your childhood friend?
ADAM. Made up.
JANET. The Willoughbys — Charley and Dana? From the old neighborhood.
ADAM. The old made-up neighborhood.
JANET. You little shit. Even Uncle Seth from Sag Harbor?
ADAM. I always wanted an Uncle Seth. *(He moves close to her.)* Can't it just be us? *(And now they kiss. A nice, long kiss.)* Just … us.
JANET. And Ray. You wouldn't get married without Ray.
ADAM. Ray believes marriage is a global conspiracy engineered by the same people who brought us bar codes and Daylight Savings Time.
JANET. How do those have *anything* to do with each other?
ADAM. You'll have to ask the expert. *(Ray enters through the front door. He wears raggedy clothes [including a very worn cardigan sweater], an old overcoat and beat-up fedora. He has a kind of low-tech radio headset on his head, connected to an [older style] cell phone, which he wears in a kind of homemade pouch around his neck.)*
RAY. *(Full of life.)* Hello, young lovebirds! — I got my save-the-date card and THE DATE IS SAVED!
JANET. Okay, good. ADAM. Hey, Ray.
RAY. And just to be clear: I do not believe marriage is a conspiracy. *Weddings* are a conspiracy — a brutal and pervasive strategy to empty the pockets of guilt-ridden parents and tie up all the good hotels in the month of June.

ADAM. Usual? *(Ray nods as he takes off his coat and hat. Adam gets Ray his usual shot and beer [anything in a brown bottle].)*
JANET. *(Playing along.)* And who might be behind this conspiracy, Ray?
RAY. You mean to say: *Who resides in its shadow?*
JANET. Okay, sure.
RAY. I have done some thinking about this and — *(With no break in his dialogue he turns his full attention to his cell phone. Into phone.)* Yes, of course I'm still on hold — waiting to bring a little common sense to your radio show whenever this current caller can be sent back to the village that's missing its idiot — *(And now he's instantly back talking to Janet.)* You see, Janet, the American wedding industry is secretly financed by an offshore consortium of big-box bridal shops —
ADAM. *(Enjoying this.)* Lovely.
RAY. *(Overlapping.)* — And — in concert with the novelty lingerie lobby and the FTD florists — these shops use their nefarious influence to force young women into *retail retaliation* against their unsuspecting parents.
JANET. Well, you're gonna love our wedding, then: nice and simple.
RAY. But I can still wear my suit, right?
ADAM. Since when do you own a suit?
RAY. Buddy a' mine in Bethesda is an undertaker. With a little notice and a closed coffin, he thinks he can score me a real nice suit for your wedding.
JANET. Either way, we just want you — *(Ray has spied her Starbucks cup. He shakes his head in sadness and disgust.)*
RAY. *Et tu,* Janet? The pagan green goddess with the pointed crown? *Et tu?! (He lifts Janet's coffee cup.)* Has she captured you, too?
JANET. It's just coffee, Ray.
RAY. No, honey. That right there is a *cult in a cup. (Re: the cup's logo.)* Note the crown itself: seven points in all — one for each continent that she has conquered.
ADAM. *(Off Janet's look.)* This is a new one. *(Ray dumps Janet's Starbucks coffee into a trash can … and pours her a mug of "bar" coffee.)*
RAY. Note the snake-like hair — she wears nothing more. The pagan purveyor of liquid arousal, she is Eve and she is the Serpent and though you may travel the whole of the earth, you shall never escape her Garden. *(Ray hands her the mug.)* Don't give in, Janet. *Be strong. (Janet dutifully lifts her mug —)*

JANET. Cheers. *(And drinks. The bar phone rings. Adam answers it.)*
ADAM. *(On phone.)* Tavern. *(Listens.)* Yeah, we're here. Haven't torn us down yet. *(Adam hangs up the phone.)*
RAY. So: I want to know every last thing about the wedding. Will there be an ice sculpture? Some little mermaid with punch flowin' over her titties?
JANET. We'll see. ADAM. Jesus.
RAY. Shoulda had one a' those when I married Doris. Woulda made all the difference.
JANET. How is Doris?
RAY. She's doin' great — best ex a man could have. I happen to know she's very happy with her new — well, what would you call it? — Her new …
ADAM. Mate? Husband?
JANET. Partner? … Wife.
ADAM. She has a new wife?
RAY. No, I believe this is her first. The first wife she's had.
JANET. Ray, you never said anything —
RAY. Anyway, they're very happy and they found a state that would give 'em a license and they kissed and ate cake and went off snorkeling in Cabo — and so now they are wife and wife and I personally think it is just downright friggin' peachy. *(And now Ray is instantly back on his cell phone. Into phone.)* AM I ON? Okay, good. First of all, the question is not, "Was the election rigged?" — The question is, "Who RIGGED IT?" — Who was behind all those hanging "chads" and all that Floridian hysteria? Who was it that managed to keep the sainted Al Gore out of the White House? Well, it was obviously the OIL MEN. They clearly rigged the election — not to put Bush in the White House, but to put Saint Gore on the road toward his Nobel Prize and the Most Convenient Truth imaginable: scaring the people into "saving the planet!" Big Oil has hypnotized the American consumer into thinking that *they alone* can save the melting ice caps by recycling their tuna cans and making their kids wear hemp! It's *outrageous* and it's *ingenious — (And now Ray is headed toward the bathroom —)* because the moment the "average person" thinks they can "make a difference," at that moment Big Oil is always *off the hook!* So — *(Until, still talking on the phone, he vanishes. Beat.)*
JANET. Adam.
ADAM. Hmm?

JANET. Don't let Ray make a toast at our wedding. *(Adam smiles and plops his backpack onto the bar — takes out a large book, legal pad, highlighter, etc. — and begins to study.)* Remember Margaret and Rachel? At the foundation?
ADAM. Mm-hmm.
JANET. They've been telling me things I need to do before the wedding. Just suggestions.
ADAM. Mm-hmm.
JANET. Like have an affair.
ADAM. *(Not looking up.)* And how did it go?
JANET. See —
ADAM. Anyone I know?
JANET. — I knew you'd make a joke.
ADAM. *(Laughs.)* Well, what do you want me to —
JANET. I knew you'd think that was really funny — but they weren't joking. They said I'd regret it if I didn't do it.
ADAM. Really?
JANET. *(Lightly.)* Because you did it. Or you will. The groom always has a final fling, right? Or wants to. *(He looks up at her.)*
ADAM. Why do you listen to these women?
JANET. I don't.
ADAM. Good. *(She kisses him.)*
JANET. How was your meeting? *(Off his look.)* With your professor.
ADAM. Former professor.
JANET. She left Columbia?
ADAM. Yeah.
JANET. What's she doing now?
ADAM. She's working in D.C. Was here to do some recruitment, I think. I'm not sure.
JANET. She met with a group of you.
ADAM. Just me. We had lunch. She has some people she'd like me to meet in D.C. Might lead to something after I get out of school.
JANET. That's great.
ADAM. Mm-hmm.
JANET. Why you? *(Off Adam's look, lightly.)* Don't take this wrong — but why'd she only meet with you? *(And Ray bounds back into the room, still talking on the phone — on the very same topic.)*
RAY. *(On phone.)* — Okay, well, true enough! — it's like believing in the (quote) Loch Ness monster or that we actually (quote) put a man on the moon — yeah, right, it's a cute idea, but — *what? (Ray*

listens on the phone, as —)

JANET. *(To Adam.)* He doesn't think we put a man on the moon?

ADAM. You should ask him.

RAY. *(On phone.)* Yeah — uh-huh —

ADAM. But when you do, make sure you're sitting down. *(Adam returns to studying. Janet opens her bag and removes a stack of wedding invitations and an address book. She sits at a table and begins to address, seal and stamp the invitations.)*

RAY. *(On phone.)* — Right — but listen to me and write this on your forehead so you'll see it every time you shave: *The planet does not need to be saved.* The planet is not *in danger.* The planet is going to be *FINE,* thankyouverymuch, because *the planet does not even know we are HERE. (To Janet.)* These are *lovely.*

JANET. Thanks.

RAY. *(Immediately back on phone.)* The planet is a spinning ball of ROCK! The planet is not *nostalgic:* She is not going to feel bad about losing some ice caps and redwoods and billions of people. The planet is not *vain:* She does not require little lakes and trees and chirpy children to make her feel *attractive.* The kicker is that all these doomsday do-gooders have got it BACKWARDS: *They need the planet — they need Mother Earth to SAVE THEM! — and just what the hell's in it for HER?! (Quick, cool.)* I'll take my answer off the air. *(Ray ends the call.)*

ADAM. *(Re: the phone call.)* All in a day's work, huh, Ray?

RAY. Vigilance, Adam. Eternal vigilance. And, hey, some guy heard my theory about Yoko Ono and the Bay of Pigs, and he wants me to do a *blob.* What's a *blob,* anyway?

JANET. A *blog.* It's called a —

ADAM. Set you up?

RAY. *(Sagely.)* I would seek to understand a beer, yes. *(Adam gets him one, as — Ray pulls a chair up next to Janet, and begins helping her with the invitations — stuffing and licking envelopes, affixing stamps. In no time, the two of them are a model of efficiency.)*

JANET. *(To Ray.)* So, where you living now?

ADAM. He's back upstairs.

JANET. No.

ADAM. *(To Ray.)* In what — 801?

RAY. 603 — not that it's any business of yours.

JANET. Ray, you can't keep staying up there —

ADAM. Forget it — he won't listen —

JANET. *(Overlapping.)* — The hotel's all boarded up! It's nothing but trash and rats and broken windows —
ADAM. If he wants to be a vagrant, just let him —
RAY. I am not a vagrant —
ADAM. Yeah, okay.
RAY. — I am an *itinerant homesteader* —
JANET. But, Ray —
RAY. — And I'll have you know that the now-defunct Yankee Hotel is the finest home I've ever had — and until that wrecking ball comes, I intend to frequent its hallways and commune with its ghosts and what's more, the rats are not bad at all on six. They're much worse right above you here — on two or three they're real thick. Like *a shimmering grey carpet.*
JANET. You could stay with us.
RAY. You're not serious.
ADAM. No, she's not.
RAY. *(To Janet.)* They must love you at that foundation. When are they gonna put you in charge of the whole shebang?
JANET. No time soon, I don't think.
RAY. Want I should talk to them?
JANET. *(Sweetly.)* Maybe not.
RAY. *(Re: Adam.)* And what about him? When he finally escapes with his fancy degree, what's he gonna be?
ADAM. Ray —
RAY. Diplomat, do-gooder, politician or spy? *(Janet laughs, as Adam says —)*
ADAM. Why do you always —
RAY. What the hell else are you gonna do with a master's in "International Studies" — *Mop the floor at the U.N.?*
ADAM. *(Light.)* What do you think I should be, Ray?
RAY. Careful. I think you should be careful. And whatever you do, and wherever you go: *Make damn sure you send me a postcard, okay?*
ADAM. Okay. *(Adam goes back to his books.)*
RAY. So, what about your thesis? — Did you finish it?
ADAM. Not yet.
RAY. What's it about? — You've never told me.
ADAM. You, Ray. It's all about you.
RAY. *(Laughs.)* Yeah, right. *(Turns to her, inquiring.)* Janet?
JANET. I'm sworn to secrecy.
RAY. Fair enough. He swore me to secrecy once.

ADAM. Ray …
RAY. About this professor he had a crush on. That sexy, Middle Eastern lady — what was her name? — Dr. Handjob, or something.
ADAM. Dr. *Andjata,* and she —
RAY. He'd get a little whiskey in him and go off on her tight blouses and short, summery skirts.
JANET. He had lunch with her yesterday.
RAY. She's still around?
ADAM. No.
RAY. Forced out by the dean, huh?
ADAM. No, she —
RAY. Deflowering the students, was she?
ADAM. — She took a leave of absence.
RAY. Uh-huh.
ADAM. She went to the NSA as a translator — a "contract linguist" —
RAY. Very cunning.
ADAM. Her job was to read and translate the "intercepts" —
JANET. The what?
RAY. It's called "chatter."
ADAM. — The messages from suspected terrorist cells —
RAY. And here comes Dr. Handjob, our little Farsi chatterbox!
ADAM. Dr. Andjata left a great job at Columbia — stepped forward to help her country — and say what you want, I *admire that,* Ray.
RAY. Hey — I was a young man once for a couple of days and I remember what I "admired" about older women.
ADAM. Her COURAGE, okay?! That's what it was. We had these debates in her class — in this "revolutionary thought" unit — about Islam and the West — and those debates were … *(Looks at Ray, at Janet.)*
RAY. No, go ahead.
ADAM. … *Thrilling.* Okay?! That's why I busted my ass for that scholarship — just to be in that room — the way people wrestled with issues, political doctrines — and it wasn't just *rants,* Ray, it was *engagement* — it was fierce, it meant something — and it was —
RAY. — *Thrilling.*
ADAM. You know what —
RAY. That's your word.
ADAM. — I'd love for her to meet you, Ray.
RAY. Why's that?

ADAM. She could *rip you a new one* in half a dozen languages. *(Adam gathers/packs up his books, etc. — and busies himself behind the bar.)*
JANET. *(To Ray.)* You don't think we landed on the moon?
RAY. *What?*
JANET. Adam said —
RAY. What kind of crackpot accusation is that?! Of course we landed on the moon. I've got a moon rock in my coat pocket!
JANET. That's impossible — ADAM. Yeah, right —
RAY. And sometimes — when the moon is completely full — that rock starts to glow, and gets real warm in my hand. Once, on All Hallows' Eve, I was able to fry an egg on top of it. *(Off her look.)* You don't believe me? Gimme an egg. Hey, Adam — you got an egg?
JANET. So, you don't think it was staged? The landing on —
RAY. Oh, the stuff on TV — which I *loved,* by the way — of course that was all staged. Everyone knows that. Buddy a' mine did the lighting for it — those neat reflections on the visors of the spacesuits — this was at an abandoned army base, outside Flagstaff. Well, as it happens, my buddy vanished shortly thereafter — had one drink too many and spilled the beans to a reporter. The reporter vanished, too. This, Janet, is a country of disappearances. *(The door opens and Palmer enters. Palmer wears dark pants, a black windbreaker. Baseball cap. His movements are calm and deliberate as, during the following, he goes to a barstool furthest away from the others. Sits. Stares front. Ray and Janet essentially ignore him.)*
JANET. So, okay — let me get this straight —
ADAM. *(To Palmer.)* What can I get you?
PALMER. Two Rocks.
JANET. It never happened.
ADAM. *(To Palmer.)* Say again?
JANET. Is that right?
PALMER. *(Holds up two fingers.)* Rolling Rock.
ADAM. Two of 'em? *(Palmer nods. Adam gets the beers.)*
JANET. No one ever walked on the moon?
RAY. Oh, sure they did. But not the moon you can see. Not the moon they write the songs about.
JANET. Then how did —
ADAM. I warned you.
JANET. — How did you get a moon rock?
RAY. From the other one. The moon we landed on. *(As Ray con-*

tinues, Adam puts the beers in front of Palmer. Palmer slides one of the beers in front of the empty seat next to him. Then: He lifts his beer, clinks it quietly against the other one … and drinks.) Keep in mind: The one we landed on cannot be seen.

ADAM. And there's the genius of Ray: You can't *see it* — so you can't *prove him wrong.*

RAY. Look: We clearly had a space program — clearly it had a purpose — and clearly that purpose was not just to plant a flag, hit a golf ball and bring home some rocks.

JANET. So what was it?

RAY. I think you can guess.

JANET. Give me a hint.

RAY. Connect the dots and the full picture emerges.

JANET. *What picture, Ray?*

RAY. If a shadow government wanted to populate a new planet and train its citizens to return one day in the future and do the sacred bidding of their American overlord, where better to begin than —

JANET. *(Playing along.)* — On this unseen moon.

RAY. *(Nods.)* I didn't believe it either, till I was given the rock. Buddy a' mine stole it from this shaman in Queens.

JANET. And these people —

RAY. Technically they're no longer "people" — they've evolved *beyond.*

JANET. — And they are coming one day to rule us from *a moon we can't see.*

RAY. Now you're talkin'.

JANET. And how many people know about this, Ray?

RAY. *(Whispers.)* Well, by my count: One more — *(Stops, re: Palmer.)* wait, *two* more people than knew about it yesterday. *(To Palmer.)* Mum's the word, buddy. *(Palmer says nothing.)* See: it's like the whole JFK thing —

JANET. *(Dismissive.)* Yes — we know — everyone has a "theory" —

RAY. *(Nods.)* — Multiple gunmen — the CIA — all those grassy knoll shenanigans —

JANET. Right.

RAY. — *What a CROCK. (Both Janet and Adam turn to Ray.)*

JANET. You're saying there was no JFK conspiracy?

RAY. *Are you kidding?!* One gunman — a couple bullets from a book depository — boom: case closed. No: The real conspiracy was the *conspiracy itself.*

ADAM. *Come again?*

RAY. Oh, the brilliant persuasion! — orchestrated by hands still unknown to this day! It is the mother of all conspiracies: When an entire nation is led to believe something *completely different* than the thing they have *seen for themselves!* And the raw genius of that strategy changed the world. Not because a promising young man with good hair was taken out in his prime, but because — from that moment on — *this country never again trusted its own eyes and ears. (Ray drinks. Janet stares at Ray for a long moment — then lifts some of the cards.)*

JANET. Where did these names come from? These made-up guests. *(Ray says nothing, turns to Adam.)*

ADAM. Sorry.

RAY. *(Direct, to Janet.)* They're not "made up." I see those people every night, right here in the hotel. Movin' through those rooms. Women who died in childbirth — still walkin' the halls, lookin' for their babies. Mob guys who got whacked along with their mistresses. Rich old coots who died in bed with all their money in the mattress.

JANET. *(Bothered by this.)* Why would you do that? For our *wedding?* Why on earth —

RAY. Nothin' to worry about, Janet — these ghosts are good people. They show up on time. And they don't eat much. *(Janet stares at him, hard. When she looks back to Adam, he is smiling.)*

JANET. Is this *funny* to you?

ADAM. No, I'm sorry — it's —

JANET. Because I have been doing *everything,* okay? All the planning, all the —

ADAM. But it's what you *want.*

JANET. — I took the morning off from work — I came here, so we could —

JANET. *Do you want to go through with this, or not?*	ADAM. Janet —
If you *don't* want to — *fine*	Of course I —
— just have the guts to *tell me.*	

(Janet pointedly throws all the invitations back into her bag —)

ADAM. Janet ... *(And heads into the bathroom. Ray turns to Palmer.)*

RAY. *(Re: Janet and Adam.)* Lovebirds. Big day's comin' up. And I'm gonna look great. Wearin' my suit and drinkin' punch from the icy nipple of a mermaid. *(Palmer does not turn, does not speak. To Palmer.)* So … *(Re: the two beers.)* who's your buddy? *(Palmer says nothing.)* Just wondering. Never seen the two of you in here before. *(To Adam.)* Barkeep — you can set us up. Another round for me, this fella, and his imaginary friend.

ADAM. *(To Palmer.)* You gotta forgive Ray — he sleeps with rats.

RAY. I'm just makin' chit-chat.

ADAM. What about all your "friends" upstairs?

RAY. Hey — the dead have got to sleep somewhere. And I did not make any of 'em up. Believe me: Most of these are people you would never *willingly invent.* So, give this man another round and put it on my tab.

ADAM. You don't have a tab.

RAY. Then put it —

ADAM. You drink for free.

RAY. — In the bottomless well of my enduring gratitude.

ADAM. *(To Palmer.)* Another beer? *(Palmer shakes his head "no." During the following: Janet reappears, takes her coffee, and moves to the [broken] jukebox — leans against it, reading the song titles within. She does not look at Adam.)*

RAY. *(Smiles, undeterred.)* Suit yourself. But keep in mind: This place has seen it all. Back in the day, this place was not just a bar, it was a *destination.* It was on the *map.* My buddy Vince — Adam's father — he'd get mail from all over the world, addressed to: "Vince. Yankee Tavern. New York City." That's all it took. This place was *known.* And Vince, God love him, he kept this place goin' — from Danny Thomas to Clarence Thomas — anything important that happened in this world happened right there on that TV: Princess Di, the Berlin Wall, O.J. in his Bronco — we were right here for all of it. *(Indicates Palmer's seat.)* I was sittin' right where you are now when Ali hit Frazier and a man hit a golf ball on the "moon" and Dick Nixon got his scheming little ass kicked while Kissinger the war criminal got off with a slap on the wrist and an offer to be *the chairman of the 9/11 commission* — since apparently *Stalin and Pol Pot were unavailable* —

ADAM. Okay, Ray — that's enough —

JANET. *(Re: jukebox.)* Did this thing ever work?

RAY. Kick it. See what happens.

JANET. No, I'm —

RAY. Give it just one good kick.

JANET. It's no big deal, I just —
RAY. That jukebox, worked perfectly fine until a Tuesday morning five years ago. It stopped playing at exactly 8:46 A.M. — at the moment the first plane hit the first tower … right in the middle of a song … and it's never made another sound. *(Ray drinks. Janet is staring at him.)*
JANET. *I try,* Ray. You know that? Sometimes I really try. Adam just laughs you off, but sometimes I think if I really hang in there and listen to your stories I'll get a little glimpse of *something,* you know? — something that might have some *shred of possibility* to it. But, you are just unbelievable!
RAY. Because you are *unable to believe. (With quiet passion.)* I knew, Janet — when that jukebox stopped — right in the middle of my wife's favorite song — I knew right then, knew it in my gut that my Doris was gone. See, the thing is: She took the number nine train to Rector Street at 8:30 every morning — walked up to the Trade Center plaza, bought a *Daily News* and a muffin. Blueberry. Every last day. Creature of habit, my ex. And why should this Tuesday morning in September be any different? *(Beat.)* The phone rang — just as she was trying to leave. Made her late. And she *missed her train.* Pure dumb luck, she said. The gods playin' dice. *(Beat.)* My Doris was spared. And she moved on, without me. *(Re: jukebox.)* And this thing … it ain't worked since. *(Ray moves to the jukebox. Beat. Then — Ray kicks/pounds the jukebox once, with force: Nothing happens.)*
JANET. *(Quiet.)* You never told us.
RAY. Didn't I? Well … no matter. *(Adam brings the coffee pot to Janet, and starts to refill her mug.)*
ADAM. Hey, maybe tonight we could —
JANET. *(Casual.)* So, Dr. Andjata wants to take you to D.C. *(Off his look.)* You thought that would slip by me?
ADAM. It's no big deal —
JANET. It's for work, right?
ADAM. — Yes —
JANET. Some kind of job interview?
ADAM. *(Nods.)* — A meeting, a couple meetings, yes —
JANET. And what's the job?
ADAM. These are contacts in the agency, the intelligence divisions — she can't just tell me the names of these people —
JANET. Oh, sure, right.
ADAM. Janet, *you know how this works.*

JANET. She can't tell you what she *does* —
ADAM. I told you what she does.
JANET. *(Overlapping.)* — She can't tell you who you're going to *meet with* or what she wants from you — all this *mystery, Adam* —
ADAM. There's no mystery!
JANET. Fine: I'll ask her myself. Will she be at graduation? *(Adam stares at her, moves away.)*
RAY. That's gonna be a great day!
ADAM. Yeah, well —
RAY. Another chance to wear my suit!
ADAM. — Don't worry about it.
RAY. C'mon, your dad would want me there! — standin' in for him. Your dad was my best friend on Earth, Adam.
ADAM. Yeah, well —
RAY. He'd stand right where you are now — sipping on a mug of Irish coffee — *(Ray points to a beat-up mug which sits in a prominent place behind the bar.) That one,* that mug right there, that was his — and that man made an Irish coffee could peel paint from a water tower —
JANET. Let it go, Ray.
RAY. *No — I do not let things go!* His dad would say to me: "Ray, I've spent my life behind bars — pourin' drinks and makin' the world blurry. I don't want that for my kid. I want my kid to make it *clear.*"
ADAM. Well, that's not gonna happen.
RAY. You tellin' me you're not gonna sell the bar?! —
ADAM. Nobody wants this dump.
RAY. — 'Cause that's what he wanted you to do! Sell this place and get the hell out. Just last week your dad was tellin' me this — he and I were talking, upstairs —
ADAM. You were *what?!*
RAY. — I SEE HIM UPSTAIRS, Adam. And we chew the fat — he's my best friend — you got a problem with that?!
ADAM. He's DEAD, Ray.
RAY. Of COURSE he's dead — that's what I'm sayin'. He's up there in his room — not always, not every night — he moves around — where he goes I don't know, it's none of my business — but I see him from time to time. He kept a room up there, you know — those years when things were rocky with your mom —
ADAM. He "kept a room"? — when was this?
RAY. — Hey, I don't like Memory Lane any more than you do,

but those were some tough days for him —
ADAM. Why would be keep a room up there?!
RAY. — And maybe he had someone he wanted to be with in that room, *and maybe this someone was a woman —*
ADAM. What the hell are you — ?!
RAY. *(Overlapping.)* — And so nowadays as he walks the halls of his own afterlife, I guess it must comfort him to come back to that room every now and again. I see him at the window up on eight. Smokin' his Chesterfields. Countin' the pigeons. You should go up and visit sometime. *(Hard beat. Adam stares at Ray, then gets right up in his face.)*
ADAM. You're done, okay? You're off the hook.
RAY. What is that supposed to —
JANET. Adam, please don't do this —
ADAM. *(Overlapping.)* Whatever promises you made to my dad — statute of limitations, okay? Time's up — I release you from ALL OF THEM —
RAY. YOU DON'T GET TO DO THAT! I watched 'em carry your father out of this room —
ADAM. He did not kill himself, okay?! I don't care what the police say —
JANET. *(Imploring.)* It's over — let it be —
RAY. There was no sign of foul play —
ADAM. There were two shots — a window was broken — there's all kinds of things that —
RAY. But, there was no money missing — there was *NOTHING MISSING AT ALL —*
ADAM. It was NOT A SUICIDE. He would never have done that.
RAY. Adam, it was his *own gun* — the one he kept behind the bar —
ADAM. Jesus, Ray —
RAY. *(Points.)* — The *one you STILL keep behind the bar!*
ADAM. — EVERYTHING *ELSE* IS A CONSPIRACY TO YOU — but the death of your best friend is *CUT AND DRIED?*
RAY. ASK HIM! — GO UP THERE AND —
JANET. *(Firm, to them both.) THAT'S ENOUGH. (Silence. Breath. Truce.)*
RAY. *(Change of tone.)* You know what I wish? Wish I could find the dartboard. Your dad had that great old dartboard. Whatever happened to that thing?

ADAM. *(Flat.)* And you said nothing was missing. *(Ray stares at Adam … then begins digging around behind the bar, looking for the dartboard. Janet is staring at the room.)*
JANET. How will they do it?
ADAM. Hmm?
JANET. When they tear this place down. Said it could be in a month or two, right? — *(Adam nods.)* Once the judge rules on it. Can't be soon enough for me. But how will they do it?
RAY. Well, an old place like this, chances are …
PALMER. *(Flat, staring front.)* They'll *pull it. (They all turn and stare at Palmer. Having said this, Palmer turns away, nurses his beer, and seems to pay them no further attention — till noted.)*
RAY. Whaddya know: *It talks.*
JANET. You mean implode it?
RAY. That's exactly what he means, right fella? "Pull it" — like they did Building Seven.
ADAM. *(Knows where this is headed.)* Oh, no you don't …
RAY. I was talkin' about this at a book signing just the other day. Little basement shop on East Third, run by a coupla student radicals who think I'm catnip in a cardigan. I was in there signin' books.
JANET. Signing what books?
RAY. Some paperback thing. 'Bout yay-big. The author never showed, so I sat down at the table and started signin'.
JANET. Signing *other people's books?*
RAY. Had to do *something* — the line was out the door and down the block — so I did my bit. People shook my hand, poured their hearts out.
JANET. And no one knew?
RAY. Can I help it if I look exactly like a big-time radical writer?!
JANET. And what was the book?
RAY. No idea. The cover was sorta red and gold — *(Janet looks at Adam ["Is this for real?"], and Adam just lifts his hands in mock resignation, as — Ray triumphantly produces something he's found in the room: an old wooden box containing some battered darts.)* And lookee here: I FOUND THE DARTS! Anyhoo: At the book signing a kid told me he'd heard me on the radio, talkin' about the "War on Terror" — God, what a beautiful phrase that is! — I bow to the sheer devious wonder of it! — Because you and I both know we can no more fight a "war on terror" than we can *"box with anxiety"* — BUT THAT'S THE GENIUS OF IT!

JANET. You were talking about the book —
RAY. See: You can fight a war against a SCARY FEELING for as long as it suits you — and then declare victory ANY TIME YOU WANT, saying, "I don't know about you, but I think the scary feeling has pretty much gone away! War over!" Anyway, this kid tells me he's gonna write his *dissertation* on me and my search for the true story behind the collapse of Building Seven.
JANET. Building Seven at the site?
ADAM. Janet, *don't.*
RAY. People forget that although TWO buildings were hit by airplanes on that terrible morning, there were THREE buildings that fell to the ground. And the third one to fall — Building Seven — World Trade Center Seven — had received only, quote, "minimal damage," and had no more than "a few isolated fires" — AND YET —
ADAM. "And yet" — here we go!
RAY. AND YET: At 5:20 P.M. on the evening of 9/11, Building Seven suddenly collapses in *the most goddamn perfect fall that you have ever seen* — a fall that remains *perfectly inside the footprint of the building* — a fall that looks to all concerned — including Dan Rather (who gave me this sweater, by the way) — looks to be the perfectly executed *demolition* of a forty-seven-story building. Gravity, man: It's not just a good idea — it's the *law.*
PALMER. *(Still quiet.)* Makes you wonder.
RAY. Damn right it "makes you wonder." Makes you wonder why the police move reporters out of the area in the late afternoon, telling them "Building Seven is going to fall" … and while the reporters are wondering, "how the hell do they know that?" *It falls.* And in doing so, it *makes history.* Because, you see: *Never in this known world has a skyscraper failed due to fire. NEVER.* Buildings of that size around the world have burned for days — *weeks even!* — but not a single one has ever fallen, until *this day* in New York City, when NOT ONE, but THREE skyscrapers will fall — to which you are going to say —
JANET. They were hit by *planes,* Ray.
RAY. — And I am going to remind you that they were *designed for that!* — designed to, quote, "withstand the impact of a jetliner" — and that is why the official report declares that *it was the FIRES and NOT THE PLANES that caused the steel to fail and the buildings to collapse.*

JANET. Because of the heat —
ADAM. Janet —
JANET. — All the jet fuel burning.
RAY. Yes, but that fuel burns no hotter than fifteen hundred degrees, while the melting point of steel is *twenty-seven hundred* — so we seem to have *a disparity,* don't we? — Which can only be solved by taking a good look at the fallen steel. Let's do it! Let's have a look at the steel! *(He downs his shot.) It never happens.* The steel is immediately hauled away and sold overseas for scrap. And when the investigators try to do their job, they are *forbidden access to Ground Zero.* Granted. At the towers there is the rush to find survivors — but at Building Seven — which has been fully evacuated — *what in God's name is the hurry?*
ADAM. Jesus, Ray — does it ever end?
RAY. Ask the guy who plugged Jimmy Hoffa — DOES IT EVER END? *I think not.*
JANET. Not everything gets known, Ray.
RAY. Oh, honey: That's where you're wrong. Because here comes Larry Silverstein! Silverstein owns the towers, he owns ALL the Trade Center buildings — and he goes on TV right after 9/11 — and this is what he says about Building Seven — quote: "I said to the firemen, 'We've had such terrible loss of life. Maybe the smartest thing to do is *pull it.* And they made that decision to *pull* and we watched the building collapse.'" *(Beat.)* Now: We all know what *"pull it"* means — *(To Palmer.)* don't we, fella?
PALMER. Roger that.
RAY. To "pull" a building is to *bring it down with explosives* — and this makes Larry Silverstein the only person on earth to admit that one of the fallen towers was imploded —
JANET. So what if it was?
RAY. *(Nods.)* Right — maybe it was more damaged than we know —
JANET. Yes — maybe it was safer to bring it down this way —
RAY. — And this is a fine theory, but for the fact it takes *two weeks* for demolition experts to prepare the charges in a building of that size — but this building is pulled *seven hours* after the attacks. So, how do they *get it ready?* And how does *no one see them?*
ADAM. *(Not looking up.)* Maybe they're invisible — like the *moon. (Ray finds a can of spray paint —)*
RAY. *(Ignoring Adam.)* If the building was pulled, then the charges had to have been placed *weeks earlier* — and if the charges were

placed weeks earlier, *who placed them and why? (Ray stands before the one large, open wall in the room —)*

ADAM. Maybe Santa Claus, the Easter Bunny, the Tooth Fairy —

RAY. And if charges were placed in Building Seven and it was *"pulled"* —

JANET. *(Joining in, not mocking.)* — Then why should we not believe that charges were *also placed in the towers?* —

RAY. — *Which fell in the same, perfectly inexplicable way?! — YES! (— And now, as he talks, Ray spray paints three very large, concentric circles on the wall — making a large "target.")*

JANET. *(Strong, prompting him.)* And what about that insurance policy?

RAY. *(Nods, on a roll now.)* That *3.5-billion-dollar* insurance policy that Silverstein took out on the Trade Center buildings just two months before 9/11. Probably just *a coincidence!*

JANET. And the primary leaseholders at Building Seven —

RAY. — Who just happen to be the FBI, the CIA, the Secret Service, the Department of Defense, the IRS, the SEC —

JANET. — And all their files on the Enron case!

RAY. More coincidence, I'm sure! And finally, it must be a TOTAL COINCIDENCE that one of the directors of the company in charge of security for the Trade Center site is a man named —

JANET. *Marvin Bush* —

RAY. — Whose brother just happens to be —

JANET. — *The President of the United States.*

RAY. *(Finishing the "target.")* ATTA GIRL! Now we're talkin'! *(Beat.) Hey: Where'd you hear all this stuff?*

JANET. It's all in Adam's thesis.

ADAM. Janet —

JANET. His professors are wild about it. There's talk it may turn into a book. *(Beat. Ray turns to Adam …)*

RAY. *(Beaming.)* You little devil! Keepin' something like that from me. Well, you can SET US UP. I'm buyin' a round for everyone — *(Re: Palmer.)* including the chatty brothers here — *(Quickly, to Adam.)* C'mon, let's get the hooch goin'! And this being a major occasion, I'm going to have my drink in your daddy's mug — *(Adam does not move. Ray gets the mug down from its place of honor —)*

ADAM. Ray, listen —

RAY. *(Overlapping.)* — Since I know he'd want me to make a toast to his son. *(— And pours some whiskey into it.)*

ADAM. — These things you say, the claims you make, on some level they *count* — they have an effect —
RAY. *(Loving this.)* Oh, you bet they do!
ADAM. — And they are not harmless.
RAY. Yes! — I'm so glad you see that — I always knew you understood!
ADAM. However bizarre they sound to others —
RAY. *(Nods.)* Oh, they of little faith!
ADAM. — The fact is — if you really want to know — these wild theories actually *do as much damage as the events which triggered them.*
RAY. Whoa whoa whoa —
ADAM. It's true that Oswald shot Kennedy — but the shot that mattered was fired by the conspiracy nuts: They shot holes in the official story and thus *destroyed the faith of a nation* —
RAY. What the hell kind of —
ADAM. *(Overlapping.)* — Or in the case of 9/11: The hijackers create the carnage, but it is the *conspiratologists* — all these gutless grandstanding little headjobs —
RAY. Guys like me, you mean?!
ADAM. *(Overlapping.)* — They are the ones who foster the *real, true, ongoing terror.*
RAY. *(Livid.)* This is why you go to school? — To mock me? — To shame your father?! —
ADAM. Forget it, Ray —
RAY. *(Overlapping.)* — You're a CHILD, Adam — you are dangerously stupid about the ways of the world — the things I am telling you are —
JANET. It was all INVESTIGATED. There was a COMMISSION.
RAY. *(LOVES this.) WHAT DID SHE SAY?!*
JANET. I said it was all —
ADAM. Nothing. She didn't say —
RAY. Oh, you BET there was a *COMMISSION!* — A commission that was so "independent" that its director had coauthored *a book with Condi Rice!*
JANET. Ray —
RAY. A commission that was so "powerful" it was denied *eighty percent* of the documents it requested — A commission that was so "necessary" — that
JANET. All I'm saying — would you listen?!

the president and vice president refused to appear before it — A commission that "gathered information" and "issued a report" — but never tried to solve the crime! —

ADAM. No, he won't.

JANET. How can you say that?!

RAY. *(Overlapping.)* — They never asked the three questions that MUST ALWAYS BE ASKED whenever a crime is committed: *Who DID IT? (Throws a dart at the wall.) Did they ACT ALONE? (Ray throws another dart.)* And *"cui bono?"* — *WHO BENEFITS? (Ray throws another dart.)*

ADAM. Well, I think we know who "did it," right?!

RAY. *Do we?*

ADAM. The names of those nineteen men have been on the list forever.

RAY. Yes! — Amazingly, the customs people put out a list at *eleven A.M. that same morning* —

ADAM. They had the passenger manifests —

RAY. Wow! — You've seen them?!

ADAM. What the hell are —

RAY. That is so *neat,* Adam! Because if you've seen those lists — *you're the first.* NO ONE has ever seen the actual passenger manifests — they've never been released —

ADAM. Are you saying that the —

RAY. *(Overlapping.)* — And so how do we account for the fact that at least FIVE of these *supposed hijackers* later turned up in the Middle East: ALIVE.

JANET. Five are confirmed — the number may be as high as *nine* —

ADAM. "May be" — "might be" — listen to yourself!

RAY. *(Overlapping.)* — But hey, if we know those five men were NOT on those planes, that means that FIVE OTHER MEN WERE on those planes and just who the hell WERE THEY?

ADAM. Ray, there is no —

RAY. *(Overlapping.)* — Gee, if only we had the surveillance videos from Logan Airport in Boston — where most all the hijackers boarded — but, *WHOA, WATCH OUT, HERE COMES ANOTHER CONSPIRACY: Those surveillance videos amazingly DO NOT EXIST! (Ray throws a final dart.)*

ADAM. Even *you,* Ray — even *you* can't honestly believe that some

faction in our government engineered the entire attack to — what? — Unleash a military build-up and consolidate the power of —
RAY. *(Finishing his thought.)* — Of a floundering one-term president who had lost the popular vote!?!
ADAM. THAT IS — I can't — Ray, that is the most *fallacious* — I mean, JESUS, it's like saying *Lincoln secretly started the Civil War!*
RAY. I can put you in touch with people who are very persuasive on that point.
ADAM. LISTEN TO YOURSELF —
RAY. "GO MASSIVE. SWEEP IT ALL UP. THINGS RELATED AND NOT." That was Donny Rumsfeld's order to his staff right after the attacks — and truer words have never been spoken — because unless you DO THAT you are never going to get to the bottom of it!
ADAM. The bottom of what?! There is no bottom with you! — if it doesn't fit your theory, you change the subject and speculate about some other piece of paranoid CRAP.
RAY. Like WHAT? Tell me *one thing* you think is just a bunch of paranoid crap.
PALMER. *(Flat, simple.)* The passport. *(They all turn to Palmer.)* That passport they found. *(Beat.)*
RAY. Yes! There you go! What ABOUT that passport?!
JANET. What passport?
RAY. What passport?! Do you — What? — Are you people *marsupials?* — Do you live inside a little protective POUCH? The passport of one of the terrorists — one of the hijackers of American flight eleven — Satam al-Sugami — this man's passport is found a few blocks away from the Trade Center site —
ADAM. According to whom?
RAY. *(Overlapping.)* — And please keep this in mind: There were only FOUR PIECES of aircraft that successfully *passed through the towers and came out the other side* — and only ONE of these four pieces is from American Airlines flight eleven — and that is a charred fragment of the plane's landing gear which is found about three blocks south of the Towers … and found nearby, there on the ground …

… is *a passport.* Without a scratch on it.

Without a single corner singed by fire.

This, apparently, is the amazing magic passport: able to fly through the heart of a burning skyscraper and land safely on the other side. Unscathed by the inferno. Impervious to ruin. *(To Palmer.)* How'm I doin', fella?

PALMER. *(Doesn't look up.)* Good by me.
RAY. This is *documented,* Janet.
JANET. It's inside a bag or something?
RAY. No.
JANET. Some kind of protective sleeve?
RAY. No. Just lying there, all by its lonesome.
ADAM. What time?
RAY. What *time?*
ADAM. Yes. What time is it found?
RAY. Because — wait, lemme see — if it's found at, say, NOON, it seems *really weird* —
ADAM. Ray —
RAY. *(Overlapping.)* — But if it's found at FIVE P.M. — well, hey, then it makes perfect sense!
ADAM. I'm just asking, Ray.
RAY. I don't KNOW, Adam — I have never UNCOVERED the EXACT TIME, all right?! —
PALMER. *(Simply.)* Three fifty-three. *(Beat.)*
RAY. What?
PALMER. Three fifty-three P.M.
RAY. Where'd you get that? *(No answer. Palmer drinks.)* No, come on, you want to play ball here? — Tell me where that number came from. *(Palmer methodically takes off his battered wristwatch. He hands it to Ray.)* Bullshit. *(Beat.)* You're sayin' you were there? You were there when they found it? *(Palmer just stares at him. Sarcastic:)* Musta had some kind of clearance, huh?! — Musta been palling around with the boys from NSA and CSG and all the rest of those spooks!
PALMER. I was alone.
RAY. Uh-huh.
PALMER. And I didn't have any gloves —
RAY. Sure. *(Palmer [perhaps] uses two straws from atop the bar to illustrate this …)*
PALMER. — But I had two pencils in my pocket. And I used 'em kind of like chopsticks —
RAY. Oh, did you now?
PALMER. *(A fierce, quiet passion.)* — To lift that passport up, out of the rubble. I had it in my hand … warm to the touch … like *a limb,* like part of a man. And I open it … and see a face … a name … *(Palmer slowly takes off his cap, sets it on the bar.)*
JANET. That's impossible —

RAY. *(Quick, sharp.) Shhhhh.*
PALMER. *(Continuing.)* … And people are running — paper is falling everywhere — like the Yankees had won it again, like there'd been a parade … and I don't know what to do, so I hold that passport up in the air — *to show it to someone,* to *make someone see. (Beat.)* But no one's watching. *(Palmer reaches out his hand …)* No one at all. *(… And Ray gives him back his watch. Silence.)*
RAY. And next time you bent down, I suppose you found, what?: maybe the Lindbergh baby wearing O.J.'s bloody clothes! — I mean, hey fella, you were on a ROLL!
PALMER. I put it in my pocket. Walked away. Later, I gave it back to them.
RAY. To the authorities?
PALMER. Yeah.
ADAM. *(Enjoying this.)* How about that, Ray?
RAY. You gave it back to them?
PALMER. Right.
RAY. Meaning they had *given it to you in the first place?*
PALMER. I placed it there, on the ground — like I was told. Kicked some dirt on it. Then I reached down … and found it. *(Palmer finishes his beer. Ray is staring at him, intently.)*
RAY. *Jesus* — I really want to believe you! I possess an enormous capacity for belief — but sakes-alive, buddy, you are *off the grid now* —
JANET. *(To Palmer.)* Who were you with?
RAY. *(Laughing.)* He's not with anybody! He's delusional! —
JANET. I want to know this —
RAY. *(Overlapping.)* — He's *all CANDLES and NO CAKE!*
PALMER. What do I owe you?
ADAM. Six-fifty. *(Palmer puts money on the counter, then starts for the door —)*
RAY. *(Enjoying himself.)* Oh, c'mon fella, don't leave! — I love nothin' better than a big lie! I was all the time shoutin' to Doris: "I want the lies!" And she'd shout back: *(À la* A Few Good Men.*)* "YOU CAN'T HANDLE THE LIES." And then we'd laugh our asses right out of our pants! *(— But Palmer is gone. Janet is staring intently at Ray.)*
JANET. Where's this passport now?
RAY. It's never mentioned again! Mind you, this is the *only existing piece of evidence* that places one of the named hijackers on one of the four commandeered flights —
ADAM. Hey, don't stop there — you better remind her that "New

York City" and "George W. Bush" both have *eleven* letters in them —
RAY. *(Blithely, to Janet.)* This is what they do.
ADAM. *(Overlapping.)* — And that after 9/11 there were *one hundred and eleven* days left in the year —
RAY. They set up a straw man.
ADAM. — And that the first plane to hit the Towers (which kind of *looked* like a giant number *eleven)* was flight number *eleven* — which had ninety-two passengers and nine plus two equals —
JANET. Okay — we get it.
ADAM. And how odd that the guy found that passport at 3:53 — add it up: *eleven!*
RAY. They focus on a couple bogus theories —
ADAM. And of course, 9-1-1 (which adds up to *eleven)* is what you dial in case of emergency — but did you know its opposite, 1-1-9, is what you dial to reach Iraq?!
RAY. — *And they use those theories to discredit ALL the theories* — because this entire cover-up depends on a "negative hallucination": the American people choosing NOT to believe what is *right in front of their face* —

ADAM. Thank you, Oliver Stone. Thank you, Michael Moore.	JANET. Then just *say it:* Who's behind it?!

RAY. — like the fact that Osama bin Laden was treated by an American doctor at an American hospital *two months before the attacks* —
ADAM. You know what, Ray —
RAY. *(Overlapping.)* — And that while going to flight school in Florida, these terrorists clearly showed *great interest* in learning to FLY commercial airliners, but *no interest whatsoever in learning to make them LAND.*
ADAM. — You can take ALL THIS STUFF and invent a circumstantial *sideshow* which suggests that EVERYTHING UNKNOWN is part of some GRAND CONSPIRACY —
RAY. This is it?!
ADAM. *(Overlapping, sharp.)* — And you can claim to be *exposing something* when in fact you are *hiding something* —
RAY. This is your grand thesis?!
ADAM. *(Overlapping.)* — Hiding your own abject fear in the face of known facts —
RAY. Your great conclusion?!
ADAM. *(Overlapping.)* — Inventing these big secret forces of evil

because that assures your status as a *helpless little visionary* — a tiny patriot crying in a wilderness of your own making — *(Ray suddenly points to Adam's forehead, touching it, strong, with his finger —)*

RAY. Right here, Adam — the world is *right here. (— But Adam holds his ground.)* And, in this world — a world we can never escape — a world made of nothing but the sound of our own thoughts — in this world … you … me … your father … all of us … we are all of us *alone. (Beat.)* Be good. And be careful. *(Ray turns, moves toward the door, gets his coat and hat, and starts out. Stops. Reaches in the pocket of his coat and removes something … A rock. Presumably his "moon rock." Ray walks back into the room — in silence — and sets the rock in front of Janet.)* Who you gonna believe? *(Ray turns and leaves. Janet stares at the rock.)*

ADAM. Why would you tell him that?

JANET. Too many secrets. *(Janet stands, gathers up her bag/purse, and starts with purpose for the door —)*

ADAM. I'll see you tonight? *(Janet stops, turns to him.)*

JANET. No more secrets. *Promise me. (Adam stares, nods, and — Janet steps back into the room: to retrieve the "moon rock." She pockets it … and leaves. Adam watches her go. Then — he busies himself around the room — nervous energy — arrives at the jukebox, stares down at it … and then he pounds on the jukebox, hard, several times with his fists, just as — Palmer reappears, in the doorway.)*

PALMER. Adam Graves. *(Adam turns.)* Name came to me as soon as I left. Your father was Vincent Graves, from Albany.

ADAM. How did you know my dad?

PALMER. This place goes way back. *(Pause.)* Think I left my cap.

ADAM. Yeah, it's there. *(Palmer retrieves his cap.)* And you left a full beer on the bar.

PALMER. Yeah. That happens. Have a good trip to D.C. *(Palmer turns to go, as — lights rush to black.)*

End of Act One

ACT TWO

Noon. Three days later. Lights up fast.

Ray is in his spot, his drink in front of him. Janet is behind the bar.

RAY. *(Lightly.)* So off he went?
JANET. Yes.
RAY. Got on a train with the slutty professor. *(Janet ignores this.)* And where's he been staying down there in the land of call girls and interns?
JANET. He's got buddies at Georgetown. He's crashing with them.
RAY. You've spoken to him.
JANET. Every couple hours. Things are fine. I think he was most worried about you.
RAY. Me?
JANET. He didn't know if you'd ever gone three days without comin' in here.
RAY. Still haven't. I used my key. *(Ray shows her a key — tied to a shoelace — that he wears around his neck, under his cardigan.)* Adam's father gave it to me. This key changed my life, Janet. If for example I encountered an alcohol-related emergency, like, say, it was suddenly *noon* — or the barkeep took off for the swamp on the Potomac. *(Indicates a pile of papers.)* Busy couple days 'round here. Those are invoices from the delivery guys. I signed for everything. Restocked the cooler. Brought in the mail. And we are now the proud sponsors of a girl's soccer team. The Yankee Tavern Tigerettes. Here's a T-shirt. *(Holds it up.)* First game is next Friday. We're supposed to bring snacks. *(Stops, off Janet's look.)* What?
JANET. Do you just *wake up this way? (Ray loudly sneezes [or blows his nose] into his handkerchief.)* Bless you.
RAY. Damn allergies. *(Ray is now looking very carefully at his handkerchief and the contents therein.)* Did you know, Janet: Researchers

have discovered a previously undocumented *spore* — a little bit of pollen that will make you sneeze till your ears come loose. And this particular spore shares *no genetic material* with any other *naturally occurring substance.* This little spore flies through the air and sells *a half-billion dollars* in allergy medicine every year — and this little floating gold mine was not made by nature: No, it was made in *a lab.* My question is this: What did the Kleenex people know and when did they know it?

JANET. Will this be on your blog?

RAY. That and more. *(Drinks.)* Had a good talk with Vince last night. We still have a lot of things to hash out.

JANET. Ray —

RAY. Had to fill him in on what Adam's up to. All this nonsense with the thesis. Thing is, Janet: Everyone thinks it's like in the movies where they close the casket and the dead guy floats up in the sky and looks down on all the living people. In the movies it seems like the dead always know what's going on. What a joke! The dead don't have a clue! Vince had no idea when your wedding was — but I showed him my save-the-date card and he wants you to know he'll be there, in the back of the church, hiding behind the organist. Isn't that nice? *(Pause. She looks at him.)*

JANET. You know I don't believe you, Ray.

RAY. I know. *(Pause.)*

JANET. Maybe Adam does. *(Off Ray's look.)* He went upstairs. The night before he left. For a couple hours — walking those halls — looking into those rooms … *(Janet pours Ray more whiskey … and then pours a whiskey for herself. Ray takes note of this.)* I *wish* he'd see his dad up there. I'd like to hear what your friend, Vince, has to say to his only son —

RAY. Janet, listen —

JANET. *(Overlapping.)* — Because Adam keeps holding onto this place — *Why?* — When I met him all he wanted was to get rid of the Tavern, get the hell out — but now he won't leave — now he's just *holding on* —

RAY. The wedding will change that. You'll see. He'll graduate and you'll be married — and the two of you'll move on and get away from here and it'll be great.

JANET. I didn't mail the invitations. *(Off his look.)* I boxed them up. Put them in the top of my closet.

RAY. Janet, wait —

JANET. *I can't do it, Ray.* There's something — something's not right —
RAY. — Just give it time —
JANET. *(Overlapping.)* — Whatever he needs, or needs to do — I don't think he can do it with me around.
RAY. Listen to me —
JANET. *I've lost him, Ray.*
RAY. *(Strong.)* — No, you have *not* lost him — you have not lost him until the day you *let him go. (Beat. Janet stares at him.) I know this,* Janet. And Vince knew this, too. He could never let go of the woman he loved — and that's the thing that killed him.
JANET. Who are you talking about — ?
RAY. This woman took the number nine train to Rector every morning. She walked to the plaza at the Trade Center. Bought the *Daily News* and a blueberry muffin. Creature of habit, she was. And when that terrible morning happened, Vince was sure she was gone. *(Beat.)*
JANET. Doris…?
RAY. He asked me the next day: "Did you hear from Doris?" I said: "Yeah, Vince, Doris is okay, missed her train, stroke of luck." And he nodded. And then I told him she was gonna leave — pack up and get out of this city for good. And I watched his face fall.
JANET. You knew about them?
RAY. He told me right then. *(Indicates bar.)* Right here. And as I turned to leave, he said, "Ray — always look after my boy." Then he locked the door behind me. *(Beat.)* The next morning I used my key. And I found him lying behind that bar. *(Pause. Janet stares at him.)* Hold on, Janet. Hold onto Adam and don't lose him. *(Beat, grins a bit, trying to change her mood.)* Remember: Him meetin' you is the best thing that ever happened to me. *(Ray finishes his drink, and stands with purpose.)* Okay: I'm off to see a man about a suit.
JANET. Ray, please …
RAY. Janet, a man my size has died and I've got to save his clothes from the worms. *(As he goes.)* Love ya. Be good. *(As Ray grabs his coat and reaches the door, the door opens and in walks —)*
PALMER. *(Dressed as before.)* How're the ghosts, Ray?
RAY. The what?
PALMER. Upstairs. How they treatin' you?
RAY. My life amid the paranormal splendor of this hotel is just

none of your damn business.
PALMER. 'Cause there's a way to get rid of 'em, you know. One sure way to get rid of a ghost.
RAY. And what might that be? *(Palmer turns to Janet —)*
PALMER. Rolling Rock. *Two of 'em. (— And then moves into the room. Sits. Janet turns to get the beers. Ray stands frozen, unable to leave.)*
RAY. *(Sharp, to Palmer.)* Hey —
JANET. Ray, don't ...
RAY. — I asked you somethin'.
JANET. ... It's okay ... I'll see you later. *(A beat, then Ray turns and goes. Janet puts the beers in front of Palmer.)*
PALMER. Thanks. Don't suppose the jukebox is working.
JANET. You're welcome to kick it.
PALMER. Does that help?
JANET. Ray says that's all it needs.
PALMER. Did he ever tell you the song?
JANET. Hmm?
PALMER. Said it stopped in the middle of a song.
JANET. Oh, right. You won't believe it.
PALMER. Try me. *(A beat. Then Janet sings a phrase of the song, softly ...)*
JANET. "Bye ... bye ... Miss American Pie ... " *(Another beat. Then they both crack up, laughing.)* Perfect, right?! —
PALMER. Absolutely.
JANET. — God, those stories — the people that believe those stories —
PALMER. Urban myths.
JANET. Right.
PALMER. You know my favorite? Guy walks into his bank in 2001, on the *eighth of September* — three days before — and he has a piece of paper in his hand. Yellow, torn from a legal pad. On this paper the guy has written some words in blue felt pen. He has described, almost *exactly,* the events of 9/11 — it's uncanny — the planes, the Towers — it's all written down right there — three days before it happens. And now, at the bank, he has a woman *notarize and date* this piece of paper. And she does. And he places it in his safe-deposit box. Turns the key. Locks it up tight. And leaves. *(Beat.)*
JANET. And he's *right.* It all *happens.*
PALMER. Yes.
JANET. God, that's creepy. That's so —

PALMER. It's a good one, huh?
JANET. — There must be all sorts of those people —
PALMER. Right —
JANET. — Claiming they knew in *advance* —
PALMER. — Right.
JANET. — 'Cause how can you prove them wrong?
PALMER. You can't. And this one actually gets better. The authorities, they find out —
JANET. *(Wry.)* Whoever "they" are, right? — the infamous "they" —
PALMER. Right — they find out about this paper — upon the guy's death —
JANET. Wait, the guy *dies?!*
PALMER. Of course he does.
JANET. "Mysterious circumstances" — "cloud of suspicion."
PALMER. You're good at this —
JANET. So the guy dies —
PALMER. — And they go to the bank —
JANET. They get a subpoena, or something —
PALMER. "They" don't need a subpoena, they just *take whatever they want* —
JANET. Yeah, of course they do —
PALMER. — Because they *have to have this.*
JANET. — Because if this is real — I mean —
PALMER. This is the Holy Grail. As soon as you have this, you no longer have speculation — you have *complicity; a lead you must follow.* And so: They open the guy's safe-deposit box … and look inside … and …
JANET. It's *gone.*
PALMER. You've heard this?
JANET. No, but it *has* to be gone, right? —
PALMER. For the story.
JANET. For the myth —
PALMER. It has to be gone. Exactly. People will believe anything they have not —
PALMER and JANET. — Been given a reason to disbelieve. *(Palmer smiles.)*
JANET. That's in Adam's thesis. He talks about that all the time.
PALMER. You've been together a while?
JANET. Yes, we have.
PALMER. Lucky him. *(She says nothing. Busies herself. Palmer lifts*

his empty.) Another Rock, if you got one. *(Janet hesitates, looking at the still-full second beer.)*
JANET. Do you not want…?
PALMER. Hmm?
JANET. You still have a full one …
PALMER. *(Simply.)* That's for Mickey. Least I can do. Buy him one … and hope that wherever the hell he is, they got a cold Rock waitin' for him. *(Janet gets Palmer another Rolling Rock. He takes it, casually clinks his bottle against the full bottle … and drinks.)*
JANET. *(Quietly.)* Friend of yours?
PALMER. *(Easy, at first.)* Worked together, drank together — knew each other's shit and always had each other's back. But the funny thing … on the morning it *mattered* — the morning it mattered the most — we got separated. He was supposed to be with me, out on the streets, but he got hung up in Seven — twenty flights up in Building Seven — because the *planning,* let's just say that the planning was *less than good.* And so later that day I was holding a passport and walking toward the building that *I knew my friend was in* — and this building started to … bend … and float … and swallow itself. *(Beat.)* If not for the planning … he'd be here … Mickey'd be right here, sippin' on that Rock. *(Silence.)*
JANET. What kind of planning? *(Palmer just drinks.)* Building Seven was empty. When it fell, that building was —
PALMER. *(Sharp.)* I don't have his *bones,* all right? Wish to hell I did. Even a fragment. Even just one — because *God, how people want PROOF.* I looked — used my clearance — got onto the site, they were already hauling away the steel — and I was digging around on the pile — ON MY KNEES — *looking for a trace. A fingernail.* The tiniest of things. They found 'em at Ground Zero — they're *still* finding them — more and more bones as they dig — but right now the only proof I'VE got is this: At 5:07 P.M. I was speaking to Mickey on a secure line — and at 5:20 P.M. that building fell … and he never once reappeared on this earth. *(Pause. With an odd edge:)* What about you, Janet? Who'd you know? Who'd you lose?
JANET. That is really —
PALMER. Insensitive?
JANET. — Yes — I mean, I'm sorry, but that's —
PALMER. How dare we dine out on our grief, right? —
JANET. Look, you can't just —
PALMER. *(Overlapping.)* — But we do it. Those of us who were

here, we all do it —
JANET. No —
PALMER. It doesn't make you some kind of monster, Janet. Were you in the city that day?
JANET. Yes, but —
PALMER. See — you do it.
JANET. *(Sharp.) No — I don't! (Beat.)* I'd walk by all those people down in Union Square, looking at the handmade signs: "Have you seen so-and-so?" And, I swear … everyone *knew someone. They* all *had someone.* Someone they lost. And I *didn't. (We think she's done, but then …)* There was a consultant at the foundation. His name was Elliot. He'd be there for meetings every other week or so. I'd said hello, nothing more. And then one day someone mentioned his girlfriend. How she'd worked for Morgan Stanley, in the north tower, had tried to call him, but …

The next time I saw him, I couldn't help it, I just … mentioned this. It was so stupid — I mean, I didn't know this guy at *all,* really … and then he asked if I wanted to have coffee.

It was nice. He talked about her. How much he missed her. We made a kind of regular date of it — coffee or a drink after work, whenever he had business in the building. And it started to get … a little more personal. I mean, he knew I was engaged, I'd told him about Adam — but he said he just really liked spending time with me, and not since he'd lost his girlfriend had he felt … you know.

And then I had this thought. It just hit me one night: *He made her up.* This loss. To get all this sympathy from people — from women — and God, that pissed me off — so I went online, to the site, where the victims are listed … and I looked up Elliot's girlfriend … and she was there. She was right there. Just like he'd told me.

And right then — I know, I don't care how this sounds — right then I wanted to tell people: "I *knew someone. I lost someone.* She died in the north tower and I knew her and I've been helping her boyfriend through his grief." The next time I saw Elliot we were at a bar, in this back booth, and he tried to kiss me — I had *wanted him to,* for *weeks,* just *a kiss,* just *that much* — but when he finally did it: I was disgusted. I wanted to be sick. Because *I had NO feelings for this guy at all* — I would never have given him the fucking time of day — except for the fact that he *knew someone …* and now *I finally knew someone. Someone who'd been there. (Pause.)*
PALMER. Did you tell Adam?

JANET. There was nothing to tell. Elliot got a new job. I never saw him again.
PALMER. And so it ended that day — when you stood up, said goodbye, and walked out of that bar. *(Janet stares at him, then busies herself once again.)* I think you stayed. Disgusted or not, I think you went back to his place. *Once. Just once.* To know what it was. I would've done the same thing, Janet. Until you know what it *is* — how can you ever be *done* with it? And you're right. There's nothing to tell Adam. Over and done. *(Beat, off her look.)* And now you can't believe you told me that. Don't worry, Janet. I keep secrets for a living. *(He produces a manila envelope from his jacket pocket.)* I have some photos for you. *(He removes some photographs from the envelope, and arranges them on the bar [or table] near Janet.)* These are copies. Keep anything you like. *(Re: photos.)* Adam seems to be in good spirits. So does she. *(Janet stares at the photos.)*
JANET. Where did you get these?
PALMER. I took them.
JANET. You —
PALMER. I'm no professional, but I get by.
JANET. *(Pause.) Why? (She looks to him for further explanation … but Palmer says nothing.)* He's still in D.C. — when did you do this? *(He lifts a photo, shows it to her.)*
PALMER. Does that look like D.C.? *(She looks more closely.)* Or does it look more like New York? Lincoln Center. *(Another photo.)* Union Square. *(Other photos.)* A gallery in Soho. The White Horse Tavern.
JANET. *(Quiet, tense.)* When?
PALMER. Two years ago. Dates are on the back. *(Janet turns the photos over, looks.)*
JANET. No … these aren't real. *Two years ago …* he was her student. Two years ago she was his professor, and he and I were already … *(Her voice fades.)*
PALMER. Yes. *(Janet picks up her cell phone. Begins dialing.)*
JANET. Get out. I mean it — get the HELL out of here! I'm calling the police, so you'd better —
PALMER. No — I think you're calling Adam. You want to be told it's all a lie — even though you know better, even though you've *seen it for yourself.*
JANET. Who are you?! Goddamnit, you tell me that much!
PALMER. I'll tell you a lot, Janet. As much as you're ready to hear.
JANET. I spoke to him last night! He's staying with some friends

in Georgetown —
PALMER. — And taking the train home today. Arrives Penn Station at seven-oh-four. That adds up to eleven, of course — which I'm sure is not lost on Adam. He never made it to Georgetown. He was in Langley, Virginia — home of the CIA and a few other secret clubs — and I know for a fact that he'll be getting off that train alone.
JANET. *(Adamant.)* He's traveling back with her. He told me that.
PALMER. This was Dr. Andjata's last week at the NSA — she had to make it a productive one. Now she'll get on a plane to Karachi. Pakistan.
JANET. How do you —
PALMER. *No one, Janet — no one on earth is going to see that woman again. (Beat.)* Adam will get off that train alone. His backpack in hand. He'll come home thinking he met a few people, made a few contacts, got to spend some quality time with his ex-professor —
JANET. Adam would not do that!
PALMER. Oh, c'mon, Janet: A little fling before the wedding — that's something I think *you can relate to,* right?! *(Janet [perhaps] throws the photos in Palmer's face — but he does not flinch. Janet moves away —)* I've been watching her for two years —
JANET. Why? Because you work for —
PALMER. I don't work for anyone — not anymore.
JANET. — If she's done something, have her arrested — get a subpoena, or a — *(And now Palmer is chuckling.)* — What? — Jesus, you're *laughing about this?! —*
PALMER. *(An edge, a smile.)* I'm not really in a position to *subpoena* people, okay? I'm not going through *established channels of inquiry* here, all right?! She had *access,* Janet — access to the intercepts, *the messages sent before the attacks —*
JANET. Yes — but what does that —
PALMER. *(Overlapping.)* — She had history at her fingertips. Whatever we don't know about 9/11 — *and I don't hear ANYONE saying we know EVERYTHING about 9/11* — whatever it is, warnings that were ignored, classified info that was leaked — *she heard it all* through her headphones, in Farsi, with no oversight: She alerts her superiors only when she chooses to, and she deletes or buries anything she wants.
JANET. *Why would she do that?*
PALMER. Protecting someone on the inside, helping some group

overseas — it doesn't matter: If anyone knew about these attacks in advance, *she has proof of it. (Beat.)* The meetings were a ruse. Make Adam think the trip was legit. His backpack is the key. Inside that backpack is *a mini-disk* — 'bout yay-big, round and shiny — and on this disk are copies of the damaging intercepts.
JANET. You're saying Adam was *helping her?*
PALMER. They're ready to board the train, to come back to New York — and she tells him there's been a change of plan, she won't be joining him — gives him a gift, a reminder of their time together, just something small — but inside this gift is that mini-disk.
JANET. But he doesn't know — he has no idea —
PALMER. Maybe he doesn't — and maybe that backpack will be stolen — stolen by one of Dr. Andjata's partners —
JANET. Look —
PALMER. — The people she's passing that disk on to.
JANET. — Even if ANY of it is true —
PALMER. Or then again: maybe Adam knows *all of it.*
JANET. *That's impossible —*
PALMER. Oh, is this where you tell me he wouldn't "do anything like this"? — Because you "KNOW HIM TOO WELL"?! *(This lands. She stares at him.)* He's a skeptic, right?
JANET. Yes, *exactly.*
PALMER. *Then he's the perfect mark. (A beat — then Janet quickly rushes to grab her cell phone off the bar [or a table], but — Palmer intercepts her before she can get there. He grabs the phone.)*

JANET. Give me that! — I mean it!	PALMER. No need to call. Listen now —

PALMER. Adam's involved in this — and that means *you are, too.*
JANET. No — no, I'm not … *(Now … Janet slowly begins to move back toward the bar …)*
PALMER. *I'm not the only one following her, Janet — I'm not the only one who wants to know what she knows.* Do you understand?
JANET. *(Quiet, detached.)* Yes.
PALMER. All I want are things made *clean.* To look Mickey's wife in the eye, and tell her what I found.
JANET. Yes. *(… Until she is standing behind the bar, still listening.)*
PALMER. There's a gun behind that bar. I know that. But you don't need it, Janet. I'm not going to hurt you. *(An icy edge.)* These are just *stories,* right? And *stories can't hurt us.* Can they?
JANET. This does not happen — these things — they're like Ray's

crazy theories — they *do not happen.*

PALMER. The only way they "do not happen" is if everything — *EVERYTHING — is a total coincidence. (During the following, Palmer very gradually approaches her. Janet stands behind the bar — her hands unseen — we have the feeling she may at any moment lift the gun …)* You can't have it both ways. The moment you no longer believe that *every single thing is a COINCIDENCE:* At that moment you are admitting that *somewhere* — in the great landscape of this event — there must be *some element* of complicity.

JANET. No — I don't believe that —

PALMER. Coincidence: Three months before the attacks, commercial airline pilots lose their right to carry firearms. They've had this right for forty years, but suddenly, in June 2001, without explanation, it is revoked.

JANET. I'm not listening to this … *(Palmer gets closer.)*

PALMER. Coincidence: Two months before the attacks, the "shoot-down orders" — the authority to have fighter jets intercept airplanes which have strayed off course — this power, for the first time ever, is transferred *away* from the military and placed at the *sole discretion of the president. (Palmer gets still closer, as — Janet moves out from behind the bar … holding the gun in her hand, at her side … and she backs away, shaking …)*

JANET. Stay away from me …

PALMER. Coincidence: The *day of the attacks* just happens to be the *same day* that NORAD has scheduled the most extensive "war games" in its history — military exercises that will simulate hijackings and planes crashing into buildings — and therefore: You must believe that on the *ONE DAY, and one day only,* that *all standard operating defense procedures at NORAD have been SUSPENDED* — that JUST BY COINCIDENCE this is the *SAME DAY that the largest attack ever on the American mainland is carried out. (And now Janet lifts the gun and points it at Palmer — but he continues, undeterred —)*

JANET. *(Crying.) Stop … please …*

PALMER. *(Nearly a whisper.)* And there is one more coincidence, Janet — and, frankly, it's the hardest one to ignore: *(— As he takes another step toward her, Janet begins to back away toward the wall with the enormous spray-painted "target" on it …)* You'll need to follow the money; look at the stock market. Look at the "put options" — the highly-leveraged bets that the stock of a company is about to

FALL DRAMATICALLY — and you'll see that on the *afternoon before the attacks* there is a huge jump in the "put options" on United Airlines — a jump that is *ninety times* (not ninety *percent*), ninety TIMES higher than normal. There is also a huge jump in the "put options" on American Airlines that is *sixty times* higher than normal. And most telling of all: *There is NO similar financial activity on any other airline in the world* — only the two companies who will lose planes the next day — a fact which the business pages immediately call *"one of the most extraordinary coincidences in the history of mankind." (Janet is now leaning against the wall — against the "target" … the gun still in her hand.) Things get known, Janet.* They get written on a piece of paper and notarized and placed in a safe deposit box *three days before the attacks.* I know this … because the man who wrote those words was a friend of mine. And I've never seen him again. *(Palmer sets Janet's cell phone on the bar. With an odd, lucid calm:)* I want to speak to Adam. You need to make that happen.
JANET. And if he won't?
PALMER. He should disappear. The only way to get rid of a ghost … is to *become* one. *(Palmer goes, as — lights rush out.*

That night. Late. Adam is sitting at a table. He is wearing a suit; his tie loose. Janet stands, opposite. Adam's backpack and [perhaps] luggage/garment bag are nearby. Adam's mood is tense.

ADAM. How much of that did you believe? *(Janet stares at him.)* What that guy told you — *did you believe all that?*
JANET. How much should I believe? *(He stares at her. Janet produces one of the photographs from Palmer.)* Should I believe this? *(She puts the photograph on the table, in front of Adam.)* Or are you gonna tell me it's "all in my head"? Or that it's "all in the past" — which doesn't seem likely. Not anymore. *(Pause.)*
ADAM. It happened. I was taking her class. Two years ago —
JANET. And since then?
ADAM. Nothing.
JANET. This weekend?!
ADAM. No —

JANET. Goddamnit, Adam, you can't keep —
ADAM. — NOTHING, Janet. We did what we went there to do —
JANET. Which was *what exactly? (No answer.)* I called your friends at Georgetown. Got the numbers from your mom —
ADAM. Jesus, why would you —
JANET. *(Overlapping.)* — And they never saw you! Had no idea you were in D.C.
ADAM. I didn't see them. We stayed at a hotel.
JANET. Okay.
ADAM. In separate rooms —
JANET. I see.
ADAM. — On separate fucking floors!
JANET. Oh, that puts my mind at ease, thank you.
ADAM. It's done, okay? *It's over and done. (Pause. Janet stares: a new tactic.)*
JANET. How were your meetings?
ADAM. Fine.
JANET. How many were there?
ADAM. Three or four. *(Pause.)*
JANET. Any prospects?
ADAM. Maybe. Yes. I think so. *(Adam says nothing.)*
JANET. Sorry about your backpack. *(Off his look.)* It was stolen, right? *(No response.) Am I right?!*
ADAM. How do you know that?
JANET. It all happened — just like he said. Your backpack was stolen and then you got it back, right? — Found it in the trash or something.
ADAM. *He told you this?*
JANET. And what was missing?
ADAM. Nothing —
JANET. *Adam —*
ADAM. — Nothing but a gift. A "graduation gift" she gave me. Nothing else was taken — just this small silver case —
JANET. And what was inside?
ADAM. Nothing.
JANET. Not a little *disk?* With some *photos on it? (He stares at her — motionless. Pause. She faces him. Realizes he doesn't know. Quiet, some relief:)* You don't know, do you? Oh, God, *you really don't … (Pause.)* She was using you — passing on information —
ADAM. No, that's not —

JANET. *(Overlapping.)* — We have to tell him — when he calls — you've got to tell him you're *NOT involved — that you had no idea about ANY of this.*
ADAM. What is it he *wants?*
JANET. It doesn't matter — as long as you don't have that disk, we're safe — it's over. *(Silence. Adam keeps looking at her. And now she realizes, in fact, that he does know. Frightened:)* No ... please tell me you don't ...
ADAM. I only need a couple days —
JANET. No ... *(Janet is tearing through Adam's backpack — searching in vain for the mini-disk —)*
ADAM. I'm going to be fine — but it's better you don't know, in case someone asks —
JANET. Adam — how could you —
ADAM. *(Overlapping.)* — You can tell them the truth: that you don't know where I went.
JANET. He'll follow you —
ADAM. No —
JANET. — He'll know where you're —
ADAM. — I'll be safe — I just want a chance to see for myself —
JANET. *But you don't believe in these things! RIGHT?! It's all bunch of PARANOID CRAP, right?! (Janet's cell phone rings — she holds it up —) This is him. (But she does not answer it — she lets it ring.)* What happened, Adam?! — What did she tell you?! — *To make you want to go through with this —*
ADAM. Janet —
JANET. — Goddamnit, *you've got to tell me something! (Janet silences her phone. He stares at her. Then ...)*
ADAM. There was a man named Abu Zubaydah. He was a major al-Qaeda operative. In 2002 he was captured by the CIA. This was hailed as a great victory in the war on terror. He was tortured — waterboarded — and in less than a minute he snapped: He gave up the names and phone numbers — from memory — of three Saudi men who claimed to know, in advance, about the 9/11 attacks. The CIA gives this information to their counterparts in Saudi Arabia ... and then a very strange thing happens:

These three men *all die in an eight-day period.*

Man Number One — who has just returned from the U.S., where his racehorse has won the first two legs of the Triple Crown — dies of a heart attack at age forty-three.

Man Number Two dies in a car crash *on the way to Man Number One's funeral.*

And, that same week, Man Number Three also dies, at age twenty-five. Of what? *Thirst.* The official report says he *died of thirst.*

These three men, Janet … they are all *princes.* Wealthy, well-to-do relatives of *King Fahd,* the Saudi leader. The great friend of the Bush White House. *(Janet's cell phone rings, again. They stare at it. Finally: Janet answers it.)*

JANET. *(On phone.)* Yes. *(She listens, as Adam moves away. Begins to put things back in his backpack. One of the things Adam puts in his backpack is the gun from behind the bar. Janet registers this as she speaks to Palmer on phone, firm:)* No — Adam's gone … I don't know where. *(She listens.)* Okay … yes … I will … *(Janet ends the call, as Adam stands at the door, backpack in hand, ready to leave.)* Please —

ADAM. No —

JANET. — Go talk to him —

ADAM. Janet —

JANET. — If you do that, he said it will all go away. Like it never happened. Like all of it *never happened. (Adam looks at her for a beat, then, he heads quickly out the door —) Adam! (And lights rush out.)*

Afternoon. Five months later. The room, until moments ago, has been filled with people. Beer bottles, drink glasses, and picked-over plates of food clutter every table and the bar. The impression is that some kind of celebratory bash may have just taken place. Also: The entire length of the bar is covered with flower arrangements and flower baskets. Small notes emerge from within them. Ray is only partially visible in the open front door, saying some final goodbyes —

RAY. Okay — thanks — right — glad you were here — we'll see you — take care and be good … *(And as Ray turns back into the room, we see that he is wearing a dark suit and tie. He actually looks pretty good. As Ray starts to pick up some of the empties on the tables, the bar phone rings. Ray answers. Into phone:)* Tavern. *(Beat.)* Oh, hey, Doris — yeah, it was quite the … quite the deal. Thought we might see you here, Doris. *(Listens.)* Mm-hmm. Sure. How *is* Kathy? Good. Glad to hear it. Hmm? Oh, I'm fine. Doin' good. What? *(Re: his suit.)* Yeah, turned out nice. The dead guy was a little skinnier than me — but on the whole I look ready to be married or buried. *(Janet enters from the front door. She wears a simple skirt and sweater — not black. Her coat is on. She is carrying a large cup of Starbucks coffee. Janet moves slowly and silently to a table and sits. Sets the coffee in front of her, amid the beer bottles and empty plates. Stares front, as Ray, watching Janet, finishes his call. Pause, quieter:)* Yeah, well, good to hear from you, Doris. I'll tell her you called. *(Ray hangs up the phone. Approaches the table, and clears the bottles and plates. Janet does not seem to notice. Ray wipes the table down with a rag. He lifts her Starbucks coffee. Takes this coffee to trash can. Pours it out. Tosses the cup in the trash. Then — Ray pours a cup of "bar" coffee into a mug … brings it to the table … and quietly sets it in front of Janet. She still does not look up.)* Your friends, Margaret and Rachel. They stopped by, too. Right at the end. *(No response.)* One of the cards is from them. *(Re: flowers on bar.)* And they brought that arrangement there. Nice, huh? *(Janet stares at the flowers from where she sits.)* Girls you work with? Margaret, Rachel. *(Janet nods. She lifts her coffee mug, and takes a few sips.)* And Doris called. Sends her best. *(Ray returns to doing some clean-up.)* Real good turnout. I stopped counting at eighty-five. Most people this place has seen since the 1980 Winter Olympics. *(Beat.)* You'd be surprised to know that the "Miracle on Ice" was, in fact, orchestrated by the *Kremlin,* in conjunction with *Disney.* The U.S. won the gold, the Wall fell, the Mouse got the movie rights — *and no one ever suspected that the fall of Communism was, in truth, a communist plot.*

JANET. *(Quietly.)* Ray.

RAY. Yeah?

JANET. Not today. *(Ray nods. From a basket on the bar, Ray picks up a large stack of cards [unopened]. He sets the cards in front of Janet.)*

RAY. They loved him, Janet. We know that much. Lot of people cared for him. And not made-up people, either. From school. Guys from back home. Friends of yours, too. Just look at all these cards — all those flowers. *(Re: a large arrangement.)* That real big, pretty one over there came last night — some guy named Elliot. Don't know if that's his first name or last. *(Janet just stares at the flowers.)*

I didn't know where you'd gone. There were a lot of people looking for you. Wanted to tell you how sorry they were —

JANET. Yeah, well, *I'm sorry, too. (And now Janet is on her feet. From behind the bar she retrieves a box of "Missing Person" fliers with Adam's picture on them. She puts them on a table and begins to count/sort them into piles — all business.)* I'm sorry people came here for what was supposed to be a *planning session* — to organize what we're going to do next — we have *so many fliers that have not gone up* — How do they think we're going to find him if we don't get out there and spread the word?! —

RAY. Honey, we've been doing that for —

JANET. *(Overlapping.)* — They all want to sit here and mourn and drink and tell stories — but goddamnit, Ray, he's *out there somewhere — and I don't want to hear any more STORIES ... (Silence. Tears. She is standing now, each hand filled with fliers. Quiet, re: fliers.)* ... We have to put these up ... *somewhere ...*

RAY. *(Quiet, careful.)* We have, honey. Everyone helped. For the last ...

JANET. Five months? Don't tell me that. Everyone keeps telling me: *"It's been five months, Janet."* No one knows better than me that it's been five months ... but *he's going to turn up.* I'm not saying something didn't happen — *of course something happened* — but we should not be having *a WAKE* — God, that is just, it's just *wrong,* it's the wrong thing, Ray ... *because he is still going to walk through that door. (Long pause.)* You don't think they're right, do you? *(Pause, as Ray stares at her.)*

RAY. *(Carefully.)* You know what they found — the police talked to you about —

JANET. They *did not find HIM.* That's all we know for sure. These reporters — these newscasters — What right do they have?! — Saying maybe he killed himself — HE DID NOT KILL HIMSELF — He would NEVER DO THAT —

RAY. It's okay ...

JANET. *(Overlapping.)* — Even if that's what his dad did, that doesn't mean —

RAY. Listen now ...

JANET. *(Overlapping.)* — They just need to find that guy — the guy who wanted to see Adam — I told them, the police, everyone — *why can't they FIND THAT GUY?! —*

RAY. They'll find him — if he's out there —

JANET. *(Overlapping.)* — This is REAL, Ray — I did not MAKE THIS UP — and the thing is — it was *me* — I *told him to go. I told Adam to go there and put an end to it.*
RAY. *(Quiet, firm.)* Don't do that — don't ever do that. He loved you, Janet — loved you so much — that's the thing … that's what you need to remember. *(Silence. Now, Ray stands/turns and faces the bar … and the full effect of the flowers and cards hits him, for the first time. With his back to Janet, he pulls out a handkerchief … wipes his reddening eyes … then quickly blows his nose. Pause, quiet.)* This is not what I wanted to wear my suit for. *(Ray tries to busy himself in the room, once again …)* What now? You want I should walk you home?
JANET. No … I might go back upstairs. That's where I was — when everyone was here. Up there walking around. I'd never done that.
RAY. Nice, huh?
JANET. There's an open window on the ninth floor …
RAY. 902. The wedding suite.
JANET. … And from there, if you lean out, you can see all the way to the river. One open space between the buildings … and way out there … this sliver of blue …
RAY. Haven't even gotten to the mail. You wanna take a look? *(Janet nods. Ray gets the mail and sets it in front of Janet. She idly shuffles through it.)* Somethin' there from the Tiger-ettes, looks like. *(Off her look.)* Our soccer team. They went undefeated.
JANET. What do you know. *(She is holding a business letter.)*
RAY. What's that? From the city?
JANET. Yeah. *(Janet hands him the letter.)*
RAY. *(As he opens it.)* Okay, here goes — when's the wrecking ball coming? *(Beat, as he reads.)* Whaddya know …
JANET. Hmm?
RAY. *(Re: letter.)* The developers are headed back to court. Ghosts are safe for another year. Wow — the folks upstairs are gonna flip! Hey, you think we oughtta — *(And now Janet has found something amid the pile of mail. She freezes, looking at it.)* Janet — what is it? *(Janet holds up a "tourist" postcard of Washington, D.C.)*
JANET. *(Hopeful.)* It's from Adam … *(They both look at it — eagerly —)*
RAY. *Thank God* — what's the date on it?! *(Janet looks expectantly at the date … and then her face goes blank.)*
JANET. *(Quiet.) Five months ago.* From D.C.

RAY. Five months ... how can that be? Why would it take so long? *(In answer: Janet hands Ray the postcard. Reads address:)* To: "Ray. Yankee Tavern. New York City." *(Pause, reads, quietly.)* "Thought you'd want to keep this in the bar, up by your old buddy's mug." *(Pause.)*

JANET. *(Quiet, curious.)* Why? What does he mean by that?

RAY. *(Quiet.)* No idea. *(Ray sighs. He turns and takes a long look in the direction of the mug.)* I'm sorry, Janet. *(She says nothing. Pause.)* How 'bout an Irish coffee? Don't that sound good?

JANET. You go ahead. *(Ray moves toward the bar. Lifts the mug down from its place. Gets a bottle of whiskey off the shelf. As Ray is about to pour the whiskey into the mug — he stops, seeing something in the mug, just as — Janet suddenly stands — and, moving with purpose, she throws on her coat, grabs her purse, and fills her hands with the missing-person fliers, as — Ray removes something from the mug: a small round mini-disk. He holds it up to the light, looking at it, saying:)*

RAY. *(Re: mini-disk.)* Janet...? *(But Janet does not see it, because she is already heading for the door, saying —)*

JANET. *(Strong, with emotion.)* I don't care — I don't care what any of you say — *GODDAMNIT — (And, passing the jukebox, she kicks it hard. As she leaves:)* HE'S OUT THERE — *HE'S STILL OUT THERE SOMEWHERE ... (And Janet is gone. And Ray is holding the disk. And the lights of the jukebox begin to flicker randomly, and — in small, random, intermittent bursts — a snippet of the slow, penultimate chorus of "American Pie" begins to play. [Note: The final phrase — "This will be the day that I die" — may be stuck/looped/repeated, but should never be fully completed.] Holding the mini-disk, Ray stumbles, amazed, first in the direction of the jukebox — then to the door, where he calls off —)**

RAY. JANET? Janet — you gotta hear this! *(And the bar phone rings, loud. Ray approaches the phone, still looking at the jukebox, still holding the mini-disk. Ray lifts the receiver — into phone.)* Tavern. *(Quiet.)* My God ... *(Still quiet, intense.) Where are you? (— As the halting, random phrase of music repeats, growing louder, and — the lights rush to black.)*

End of Play

* See Special Note on Songs and Recordings on copyright page.

ON TAVERNS AND TALL TALES
by Steven Dietz

Stories are bigger at the bar.

There is something about the inherent camaraderie of tippling strangers that renders even the simple story a little bigger, a little more rigorously outlandish. The fits and starts that comprise our daily lives can — with a bottle of beer and an attentive bartender — attain in the telling a certain rough-hewn majesty.

Taverns are home to the tallest of Tall Tales, where once can be nightly rewarded with some terrific lie, boast, promise or story. The air is thick with invention.

A man, for example, can go into a bar and order a Rolling Rock beer — in its traditional green bottle. And as this man sips his beer, another man might note the odd and enduring number "33" that has appeared on bottles of Rolling Rock since the brewery's founding in 1939. This man might say the "33" signifies the year that Prohibition ended — a worthy date for a brewer to immortalize. Another man might (rightly) say the number represents the 33 words that comprised the beer's original slogan.

Still another man will say, with absolute certainty: *"The number on that beer bottle represents the 33 degrees of the Scottish Rite — the holy order of Freemasons. It's a sacred and mysterious number — part of their plan to control government and control the world."*

And then the guy at the very end of the bar will say: *"Those are the same guys who were behind 9/11."*

And some will nod. And some will laugh. And all will drink their beer. The biggest story wins.

A "conspiracy theory" is simply a Tall Tale without end. It contains all the marvelous speculative reach of a great myth — with just enough factual ballast to get the attention of the Doubting Guy across the room. And the bigger the event — the Kennedy

Assassination, the 9/11 attacks — the bigger the potential landscape; the more malleable the coincidences.

What's more: a conspiracy theory significantly raises the status of the Teller. Whereas the teller of a Tall Tale is a person sharing a story, the teller of a conspiracy is sharing a *secret*. He is "letting you in on something only a few people know about" — and thus your status as a Listener, too, is ennobled. You are special. And you are now complicit. Stories bind us to one another in insidious ways.

The surprise, terror and inexplicable complexity of the 9/11 attacks have launched a lifetime's worth of speculation. And with avid speculation — and a little canny imagining — any number of Tall Tales can be spun about "what really happened" and "who was really behind it." And most all of them are patently absurd.

Except for the ones that maybe ... aren't. The ones that, despite our rational firewall, tend to hold our attention for a minute or two. The niggling curiosity, the odd question that takes up residence in our mind.

And what do we do with this curiosity? (We can't "put it out of our mind" — despite how often that comical phrase is uttered.) So, we await *context*. We await someone who will give these questions a home — spin them into a shape we recognize — for no reason, perhaps, other than our own amusement. We wish to manage the unknown, and the only way to manage these dark and mysterious imaginings is to *make them into a story*.

And there is always someone ready to tell your fears back to you. There is always a Teller at the bar. There is always a bigger story hiding in the room than the one you brought through the door.

So, welcome to the Yankee Tavern. Take off your coat. Pull up a stool.

What'll it be tonight?

May 5, 2009
Austin

PROPERTY LIST

2 large Starbucks coffee cups
Purse with stack of returned envelopes
Older headset, cell phone
Coffee mug
Backpack with books, legal pad, pens, etc.
Stack of wedding invitations, pen, stamps, address book
Beers, whiskey, shotglasses
Old wooden box with darts
Spray paint
Old, battered coffee mug with mini-disk
Straws
Money
Rock
Key on shoelace
Papers, mail
Handkerchief
Envelope with photographs
Cell phone
Gun
Suitcase
Beer bottles, plates of food, etc.
Flower arrangements
Cards
Missing person fliers
Letter
Postcard of Washington, DC

SOUND EFFECTS

Phone rings
Cell phone rings
Music from jukebox